Smudging

By Elizabeth Wood

COPYRIGHT © 2017 BY M. ELIZABETH WOOD

All rights reserved. No part of this publication may be reproduced, distributed, or transmitted in any form or by any means, including photocopying, recording, or other electronic methods without prior written permission of the author or publisher, except in the case of quotations embodied in critical reviews and certain other noncommercial uses permitted by copyright law.

Content

1. What is Smudging? 6

2. Some History on Smudging 12

3. Common Herbs for Smudging 16

4. Some Smudging Rituals 29

5. Smudging to Remove Ghosts 38

6. Alternatives to Smudging With Smoke 44

7. Conclusion 52

Disclaimer; This book is intended for general information only. The concepts presented in this book derive from metaphysical beliefs throughout different parts of the world including ancient civilizations and folk lore. The ideas, procedures and suggestions in this book are not to be understood as directions, recommendations, or prescriptions. The ideas presented in this book should not replace the advice of trained professionals. The author and publisher do not make any claim to do more than provide information and report as folk lore. The author and publisher of this book disclaim any liability arising directly or indirectly from the use of this book.

A Smudging Chant

By light of sun and dark of moon

All Negativity must leave this room

I welcome in the warmth of love

And God's protection from above

Release this smoke to cleanse the air

And offer my home its peace and care

~1~

What is Smudging?

Smudging is when you smolder select herbs to change the ions in a space. Ions fill the air. There are positive ions and negative ions, and they are scientifically proven to have a physical effect on us.

Positive ions are not healthy. They are prominently found in areas that have a lot of negativity. Positive ions are increased in areas where people suffer from illness, depression, allergies, exhaustion or emotional distress. This is also true in areas of congestion, and cluttered spaces. Have you ever walked into a room and felt the heaviness? That's because it becomes necessary to clean the energy. Similar to dusting or scrubbing your home, or bathing your body, smudging cleanses the air in a space, around an object, or a person, with a rinse of therapeutic smoke. It is sometimes referred to as a "spiritual shower".

Negative ions are healthy. They are found in areas that generally have a lot of fresh air. Negative ions are prominently found in natural settings like mountains, gardens, beaches, waterfalls, or after a rain storm.

When you breathe in negative ions they increase the blood flow to the brain. They also increase the levels of serotonin in our systems. Serotonin is the hormone that increases energy, positive attitude, and contentment. It relieves stress and counters depression.

Test this for yourself. Spend some time in a cramped, cluttered or suppressed area. Choose a place that is filled with people who are stressed, arguing, unhappy, have allergies, or maybe a place where there is a lot of pet dander. Spend some time there and observe how you feel; then spend some time walking outside. Try to visit an area with some water, if possible. Follow a path to a stream, or visit a nearby fountain. Breathe in the fresh air and notice the difference in your mood. You will not only feel better emotionally, but physically as well.

Smudging also offers other benefits. To name a few, it can help raise the vibrational level of your space or Aura, which is important for manifesting. It can also relieve chaotic spiritual energy that may be influencing the mood or comfort of a space.

To smudge, your selections of herbs are bound together with an flammable string, making a smudge stick. The stick is burned in a fire retardant container, and the smoke is then released through the area being cleansed.

Besides clearing a room, smudging is commonly used in different practices where the benefits help achieve a goal. In the practice of meditation it is used to clear away negative energy and promote calm nerves. It is used along with Reiki, to clear away negative energy and help open the Chakras. It is used during massage, to clear a person of damaging energy and promote relaxation and good health. It is also used as a tool to help clear lingering energies before or after psychic work.

A modern smudge set consists of a smudge stick, which is your herbs bound together, an abalone shell and a feather. Each part of the set represents an element of life energy. The abalone shell represents the element of water. The unlit herbs represent the earth. The burning herbs represent fire. And the smoke represents air.

It is important that you understand the beliefs of the occult you practice, as this may cause the items of a smudge kit to vary. An example of my point is that burning herbs for ritualistic ceremonies is something that is common amongst witches. Yet when smudging in accordance with the Wiccan beliefs you should not use an abalone shell. Abalone is considered sacred to the Goddess. Shells are affiliated with water, and, because of this, not considered appropriate to use in air or fire rituals. Another consideration is that Abalone has now been added to the endangered list.

When smudging in the Native American tradition, the Abalone shell is replaced with a sacred bowl to contain the smoldering embers. Also the items of a kit are usually stored together in a leather medicine bag or wrapped in a cloth between smudging.

Throughout this book you will find a sprinkling of Smudge chants. They are only recommendations. They are not traditional, only chants that I have put together over time to help myself. Feel free to use them, write your own or research more traditional verses to use.

~2~

Some History on Smudging

The history of smudging stems from incense, which is the ancient tradition of burning herbs during a ceremony. Burning herbs for religious reasons can be dated as far back as 626 BC, to the Babylonian Empire.

Ancient Egyptians devoted altars to the burning of herbs to drive away demons, welcome their Gods and send off the dead. This is inscribed on a tablet that was placed on the Sphinx at Giza, Egypt in 1530 B.C.E.

In ancient Greece, smudging was used to communicate with those that passed on. The practice also has history in Israel, Rome and India. The Hindus and Buddhist still smudge in their rituals.

Frankincense and Myrrh, two herbs used in smudging, were included in the gifts from the three wise men to Baby Jesus.

It is historically noted that the Ancient Azteca of the thirteenth century and Maya Empire of the sixth century A.D. smudged with Pine needles.

Anglo-Saxon tribes believed in nine sacred herbs gifted to the world by the god Woden. These herbs were used for various reasons from medicinal, to pesticides, to religious.

Many Native American tribes burned herbs regularly in sacred bowls. Besides religious rituals, they smudged for a lot of physical purposes. They used the smoke of different herbs as pesticides, to preserve food, tan hides, heal the sick, and smoke tobacco.

My Broken Heart Smudge

With sacred smoke I call upon the help of spirit

I cleanse the hurt from my heart

I cleanse the exhausted from my spirit

I cleanse the anger from my thoughts

May it all evaporate with the vapors of this smoke

Or turn to ash in the embers of this sage

With the power of this ancient ritual

I welcome only light and love to fill my being

I am grateful for my new welcome peace

~3~

Common Herbs for Smudging

White Sage is the most common herb used in the modern smudge stick. It has a long history of being used as a medicine, as well as in ceremonies and rituals. It was used by the Navajos to relieve headaches and fevers. It is said to boost your energy, bless your space, bring protection, ward off ghosts and change the Ions of a space to remove negativity.

In Reiki work, or other energy healing meditations, White Sage tends to be smudged for work on all the chakras, because the goal is to clear away all negativity. However, some Reiki Masters will use White Sage when focusing in on the Third Chakra, also known as the Solar Plexus Chakra. This Chakra correlates with matters of ego such as confidence, self-worth, and control.

In Magick White Sage is burned in preparation for some of the Witches Sabbaths, of Yule, Mabon, and Samhain. It is also used as part of spell work for banishing, purging, cleansing, clairvoyance, expulsion, creative inspiration, wisdom, meditation, dreams, will power, balance, and strength.

Mugwort is also known as Black Sage. It is a powerful protector, used to cleanse areas of very heavy negative energy. A few examples would be spaces affected by drug addiction, violence, or active ghosts.

In Greek mythology Mugwort is linked with Artemis, the Greek Goddess of the moon, hunting and chastity. This links Mugwort to rituals surrounding the moon, hunting, and young women.

In Reiki and other energy healing meditations Mugwort is used in work with the sixth Chakra, otherwise known as the Third Eye. Work on this Chakra can benefit matters of the mind such as focus, intuition, imagination, intelligence, and decision making.

For Magick, Mugwort is one of the herbs associated with preparations for the Witches Sabbath of Litha. It is used in spell work for love, visions, banishing, divination, and psychic matters and manifesting.

Cedar is like a wise old man, as some types of Cedar trees can live up to three hundred years old. Because of this, it traditionally symbolizes wisdom and power. It is used to smudge away negative energy, but is also known to usher in good energy. It is a popular choice for house blessings.

Cedar is often burned while praying or setting an intention, as it is believed that the words float up on the smoke. Cedar is said to stimulate clairvoyant visions, and bring energy to an exhausted spirit. It is also considered a strong protector and can open doorways to other worlds. For that reason cedar is burned when clearing out ghosts.

In Reiki work, and other energy healing meditations, Cedar is smudged when working on the First Chakra, also known as the Root Chakra. Working on the First Chakra helps balance the survival instinct when it is over active and causing unwarranted panic attacks. It also restores matters of self-identity, purpose, stability, and our relationships with food and money.

In Magick, Cedar is used in spell work associated with Gods of the Hunter, elves, cleansing, accomplishing goals, meditation, will power, calming, and protecting.

Sweet grass can be made by braiding blades of grass together. There are different types of grass used for this. When braided the grass represents the hair of Mother Earth. Put together, the grass grows strength and is more powerful than single strands of grass. Smudging with Sweet grass should be done when dealing with a community or need to unite. It is burned after smudging to clear, and is meant to welcome in good spirits. Sweet grass is said to represent the breath of Mother Earth. It is a reminder to be thankful that the earth provides us with everything we need for survival.

In Reiki work, or other energy healing meditations, Sweet grass is smudged to open the Third Chakra, also known as the Solar Plexus Chakra. This Chakra correlates with matters of ego such as confidence, self-worth, and control.

In Magick, Sweet grass is used in spell work for blessings, deeming something sacred, reincarnation, reaching out to spirit or ancestors, and the quest for wisdom.

Lavender is the herb of love. Legend is that Cleopatra used lavender to seduce both Julius Caesar and Mark Antony. When burning, it is mixed along with the other herbs in a smudge stick. Lavender is used to calm nerves. It is also added to smudge sticks when trying to settle racing thoughts.

In Reiki work and other energy healing meditations, as it is said to open the fourth Chakra, also known as the Heart Chakra or Anahata. Matters of fourth Chakra would relate to love, happiness, peace, trust, and empathy.

In Magick, lavender is one of the herbs used in the Witches Sabbath known as Litha. It is used in spell work for blessing, happiness, peace, love, psychic abilities, protection and exorcism.

Copal is tree sap that originates in Mexico. Tree sap is the blood of the tree. This makes Copal sacred, as trees honor us with many gifts, including the air we breathe. Copal is used for smudging when purifying psychic tools, for psychic strength, and during commitment rituals. It was also burned by Maya Indians when fighting spirit possession. Copal is also a powerful aid in the manifestation of intentions. Copal should be burned on charcoal disks.

In the work of Reiki and other energy healing, Copal is known to open and cleanse all the Chakras.

Magick uses for Copal include spell work for blessings, clairvoyance, exorcism, creativity, wisdom, meditation, psychic abilities, and dreams.

Frankincense is a tree resin. It has been used in smudging for thousands of years. It was once considered more valuable than gold. It was used during the embalming of

Egyptian Pharaohs, to cleanse and protect the soul. Frankincense is smudged in areas of depression. It is also said to sharpen psychic abilities. Frankincense should be burned on charcoal disks.

In Reiki and other energy healing meditations, Frankincense aligns with the sixth Chakra, also known as the Third Eye. It is used in all matters of stimulating higher awareness, clairvoyance and intuition.

In Magick, Frankincense is smudged in preparation for the Witches Sabbaths of Yule, Beltane, and Lughnassadh. It is used in spell work for blessing, cleansing, exorcism, creativity, wisdom, meditation, strength, defense, and psychic abilities.

Myrrh is a tree resin that is believed to help energize a higher awareness. It is used to remove blocks along the path of life's journey. Myrrh should be burned on charcoal disks.

In Reiki and other energy healing meditations, Myrrh resonates with two Chakras. The third Chakra, also known as the Solar Plexus, is cleared in energy work regarding matters concerning ego, confidence, self-worth, and control. It also resonates with the fourth Chakra, also known as the Heart Chakra. Work on the fourth Chakra would relate to love, happiness, peace, trust, and empathy.

In Magick, Myrrh is included in preparation of the Witches Sabbaths of Imbolc and Mabon. It is used in spell work for purposes of cursing, clairvoyance.

Juniper Berry can be used to help clear negative energy. However it is more commonly used to usher in positive energy after a clearing. It is generally smudged in areas that need to be safe or are used for healing. It is said to detox and restore balance to a space. Juniper Berry can also be smudged when making intentions in manifestation.

In Reiki and other energy healing meditations Juniper Berry is said to help open three Chakras.

The third Chakra is also known as the Solar Plexus. It is cleared in energy work on matters concerning ego, confidence, self-worth, and control.

The Seventh Chakra is also known as the Crown Chakra. Work on this Chakra opens our ability to connect to our spirituality, be creative, and feel our true inner beauty.

The first Chakra is also known as the Root Chakra. First Chakra work helps restore balance to survival instinct, self-identity, ambition, stability, and our relationships with food and money.

Magick uses for Juniper Berry include purification before the Witches Sabbaths of Yule, and Mabon. It is used in spell work for focus and balance, clarity, and cleansing.

~A Body Cleansing~

With this smoke I send away

The negativity that blocks me

May my hands be cleansed to work and create

May my heart be cleared to love and trust

May my feet be free to get me where I want to go

May my throat be able to speak my words

May my eyes be sharp to see the good

May my mind be open to accept new things

May my soul be filled with gratitude

May the universe bring to my body only good things in only good ways.

~4~

Some Smudging Rituals

There seem to be different ideas of what is the proper way to smudge at home. As you read through these suggestions keep in mind that your intentions are the most important part of any smudge ritual. Once your intention is clear and strong you should choose the way with which you are most comfortable.

One thing that seems a constant, regardless of what tradition you are choosing to smudge in, is that before you begin it's important to clean the space. Clear away clutter because it may block the flow of energy. Dust the area, and vacuum, if possible.

Once the area is clean it's time to smudge. You must make sure the areas you are smudging have good ventilation, like windows, vents, or exhaust fans. Never smudge around infants, the elderly, anyone with respiratory issues, allergies or small animals. Never smudge around birds. Birds are very sensitive to smoke. It makes them extremely sick and may cause their death.

Some herbs do not burn as easily or quickly as others. It may take a little time to get the smudge stick burning. Remember to stay calm and focus on your intention as you work at this. A lit candle works well as it is a constant source of flame. Once there is a flame, you should choke it out so that the herbs are only smoldering. Sage, in particular, can take a lot of patience to keep lit.

There are different recommendations for how to go about Smudging. Some traditions suggest smudging in the cardinal directions, East, West, North, South, up, down and center. In this scenario you would begin at the East side of the home or space. This is symbolic of the sun rising in the East. Gently use your hand or a feather to wave the smoke in the direction you are working on. Never blow the smoke. This may seem easier, but when blowing on the smoke you contaminate it with your internal energy.

State your intention, say your prayer, recite your chant or cast your spell, as you move through the room, allowing the smoke to work its way through each of the cardinal directions. Your intention is very important here. Believe in it, trust in it, and state it with conviction.

Another way to smudge is by starting in the part of the space or home that is farthest from the entrance. As you move through each room you use the feather to wave the smoke in the direction of the main entrance. In this situation you are trying to usher the negativity back out the main entrance.

When you reach the entrance say a prayer or intention asking that the home be protected as you send the negative energy out or that the negativity be returned to its source. As you wave the smoke back out through the main door, state that the negativity may not return.

Some recommendations are that you start at the lowest point in the house, and make your way to the highest point. But move in a clockwise direction through each room as you go. After you have circled the room, you should spend an extra moment in the doorway before entering and smudging the next room.

Do not forget to smudge the out of sight areas, like behind doors, and under stairwells. If you can't remember your intention, prayer, or chant then write it down and look at it as you recite it.

If you are smudging yourself, move the smoke around your body while stating your intention. Focus on the areas of your body that have been physically suffering with pain, injury, or illness. Concentrate on areas that are dealing with mental pain, depression, a heart break, anger, blocked Chakra's, or psychic matters. Visualize these negative issues attaching to the smoke and being carried away. Use your mind's eye to watch them evaporate into the universe. If you are smudging to remove a negative presence, this is a good time to ask for protection from your spirit.

Smudging another person is handled similar to smudging yourself. It is sometimes done during a ritual, or healing work. Focus on your intention for them as you move the smoke around. As you direct smudging smoke to their place of ailment, state your intention for their healing. Visualize the negativity being carried away. Remember to smudge the Chakras.

Some common objects that people smudge are tools, jewelry, crystals or psychic instruments. You should hold the item in the smoke or place the object where it is easy to wave the smoke over it. State your intention. Visualize the negativity being carried away from it. Always state that you are thankful for this item and remember to say that you are grateful for its aid in your work or daily life.

When you are finished smudging put the smudge stick into a fireproof container filled with sand or salt and choke it out. Never leave a smudge stick unattended until you are completely sure it is no longer smoldering.

How often you smudge varies depending upon your needs and reasons. Commonly it is practiced at the beginning of each season. After a good spring cleaning it's always good to smudge. Sometimes an extra mid-winter smudge is necessary if you live in an area of long cold winters, where people are spending a lot time indoors together. There are instances where it is necessary to smudge more often. An example would be when cleansing a house of chaotic spiritual activity. Whenever you choose to smudge remember to make it an exciting ritual for yourself. I like to choose a night of the full moon after a deep house cleaning and smudge. When the moon is full the energy seems stronger, almost magical, and I feel as if the presence of my strong intention works better.

Spring Cleaning Clearing

By warmth of sun and budding of trees

I cleanse this room of heavy energy

All negative,

All stagnant,

All dark energy may not stay

Along with the winter it shall all melt away

~5~

Smudging to Remove Ghosts

Smudging with sage and other herbs removes lower energy from your space. Ghosts of beings of a lower energy form. By smudging you raise the energy levels of your area. This will make it so your space does not feel as comfortable for ghosts.

Before attempting to smudge away a supernatural being keep in mind that if you are dealing with a harmful ghost or a threatening presence, you should contact an expert in spiritual cleansing. A professional spirit release and spirit attachment practitioner will have the experience and qualifications necessary to deal with these situations. Do not attempt to remove these types of presences on your own.

Usually when you hear whispers in the air, footsteps up the stairs or feel chills down your spine you have a ghost. Most ghosts mean you no harm. They are simply lost, confused, trapped or feel they have unfinished business. Sometimes the ghost just does not realize that you do not want them around.

When you have the presence of a ghost it may be that they need assistance walking to the light. You can try smudging.

The herbs recommended to smudge for ghosts are White Sage, Mugwort, and Cedar. There are a few stages for getting rid of ghosts. First off you will simply ask them to leave. If that does not work, you order them to leave. Lastly, you may have to have the ghost banished. I do not recommend you try banishing without the help of a professional.

In each of these stages a combination of smudging and prayer is recommended. During your prayer call upon your God, goddess, Saints, angels, your spiritual advisors and ancestors to assist in keeping you safe and helping you to convince the trapped or confused ghost to go into the light. Always remember to ask for only good things, in only good ways for yourself, your family, your home and the ghost. It should not be your intention to harm the ghost. You just want them to leave for they are not welcome in your space. It may help to keep in mind that ghosts were formerly in human form. They may be an ancestor or someone you used to know.

As you walk through your home with the smudge, communicate with the ghost. It is really important to speak with confidence. Do not show fear. In stage one you can simply ask the ghost to leave.

An example of what to say would be, "I don't mean you any harm. But you should not be here. I am asking you to move on. You should go to the light. But if you choose to not go to the light, then I still ask you to leave here. I wish you well as you move on."

After a few days, if you still sense the presence of the ghost you will need to smudge again. Some ghosts are stubborn, or they may feel as though they have unfinished business in your space. In these situations you should be firm when communicating with the ghost.

As you walk through your home with the smudge this time, you are going to tell the ghost to leave instead of asking. Remember to sound confident and not afraid.

An example of what you might say would be, "You are no longer welcome here. You have no business here. Whatever you feel is unfinished is no longer important in this house. It is time for you to leave. Move on and do not return. If you go to the light you will find peace and love. But even if you do not choose the light you must leave here."

If the ghost is not convinced or not able to leave then you will have to move on to Banishing. At this point you should call someone with experience, before attempting to banish a ghost. It may be a situation where the ghost is trapped, or stubborn or spiteful. In these scenarios it is not wise to antagonize the ghost. You may not understand their reasons and furthermore you do not want to get hurt.

~6~

Alternatives to Smudging With Smoke

You can still smudge without using smoke. It is not always okay to create smoke and spread it around a room. Imagine the reaction at your office, or the danger of damaging the interior of your car. Or perhaps, you live with an infant, a person with respiratory issues, an elderly person or small animals.

It's important to make sure that you or those around you do not have sensitivities to any of the herbs or essential oils that you decide to use. Also keep in mind that respiratory issues or allergies may be aggravated by the aromas of different herbs.

Listed are some alternative options to smudging without the use of smoke. The most important part of each of the following recipes is to infuse your intention as you prepare it. Remember to be creative. Buy a beautiful spray bottle at the local craft store. Add a dried petal from that colorful flower you found while hiking. Put your most powerful crystal at the bottom of the bottle. Allow yourself to feel excitement as you prepare these recipes and always prepare them by hand. The power of your positive mood will help infuse your intention.

Cleansing Salt Air Spray:

Salt water solution is the simplest way to cleanse without the use of smoke. It is the best alternative to use when you are cleansing an area where someone has respiratory issues or allergies.

For this solution you can use sea water from the beach, melted water from a new snow, or fresh rain mixed with your favorite salt. You can also use water from your tap mixed with a few pinches of salt. Whatever salt you have on hand in your kitchen will work.

Let the solution of salt and water sit in a spray bottle until the salt is fully dissolved.

This salt water solution is a base solution, so you can add a few drops of needed essential oils to it. Just keep in mind that certain oils may stain fabrics when spraying.

Spray this solution into the air around your space, or around your body, while stating your intention. As with smudging remember to spray the dark areas such as behind doors and under stairs.

Homemade Smokeless Smudge Spray:
Mix the following ingredients in a spray bottle,
30-40 drops of sage essential oil
4 ounces of distilled water
1 teaspoon of pure grain alcohol or high proof Vodka

This smudge spray holds all the same energetic and magical properties of sage smudging.

You can also add the essential oils of other important herbs to this basic recipe.

Steam Smudging:

This is good when working in the kitchen or over a fire outside. Boil fresh herbs together, until the water simmers to a dark color.

Focus on your intention as the ingredients come to a boil. The steam from the pot acts like smoke as it carries away the negative energy in your kitchen. It is not recommended that you carry the pot of boiling water around. And always use caution when dealing with the hazards of boiling water and steam. As with cooking, never leave a boiling pot of water unattended.

Florida Water:

Florida water is known for its purifying powers. The name Florida Water comes from the mythical fountain of youth, which is located in St. Augustine, Florida in the southern part of the United States. The Fountain of Youth was first discovered in 1513 and said to have mystical healing powers.

Since the 1800's recipes have been circulating that are meant to simulate the same protective powers as the Fountain of Youth. You can use this basic recipe to create a spray to ward off negative energy and welcome protection. Adjust or add essential oils to meet your needs.

Ingredients

3 cups high proof vodka or alcohol

¼ cup dry White Sage

¼ cup dry lemon rind

1 teaspoon of dry lavender flowers or 6 drops of lavender essential oil

6 drops bergamot essential oil

4 cloves

Mix all ingredients in a jar and let sit at room temperature for two weeks. For spell work and magick the infusing mixture should be set out under a full or new moon during that two week period. Once two weeks have passed, strain to separate out the herbs and flowers, putting the liquid into a clean glass container with a lid. This mixture should be stored at room temperature.

Room Blessing

By light of sun and dark of moon

I ask for Spirit to bless this room

Take judgment and sadness and anger away

Bring comfort and peace and let it stay

Please bless our home Dear Spirit above

And fill it with only good and love

~7~

Conclusion

The most important part of smudging is to set a very clear intention. Feel what you are saying in your heart. Believe it in your mind. What you want is very simple, for the negative energy to leave. You want positive energy to come in.

If you are not sure of what to say then look around. Do research. There are many choices of prayers, intentions, spells and chants out there.

Always remember to ask for help from your spirit protectors. Start with a prayer to God, or God and Goddess, the Saints, Angels, ancestors, your spirit guide or your higher self. Their help will strengthen the power of your intention.

Most importantly, remember to be careful and use caution when smudging.

Happy Smudging! And as always, I wish you only good things in only good ways.

Printed in Great Britain
by Amazon